TIMELESS PLACES

PROVENCE

ALEXANDRA BONFANTE-WARREN

BARNES
&NOBLE
BOOKS
NEW YORK

ISBN 0-7607-4521-8

Editor: Nathaniel Marunas
Art Director/Designer: Jeff Batzli
Photography Editor: Amy Talluto
Production Manager: Camille Lee

Color separations by Colourscan Overseas Co Pte Ltd
Printed in Hong Kong by Midas Printing Limited

3 5 7 9 10 8 6 4 2

❧

PAGE 1: **Lacoste, in the Petit Lubéron, overlooks the Vaucluse. The city's most famous resident was the lord of the manor, the Marquis de Sade, who (thanks to his particular appetites) spent more time in prison than he did in his ancestral home.**

PAGES 2–3: **Vast, serene skies shelter the plains of the Rhône Valley—here, in the environs of Arles, a stone house appears welcoming in the distance...**

PAGES 4–5: **Ménerbes' solemn, almost mournful beauty reflects its history: the town, the last Calvinist stronghold in the sixteenth-century Wars of Religion, succumbed to royalist forces only after a brutal, fifteen-month siege.**

PAGE 6: **Many glorious dawns have been seen to rise over the Grand Lubéron; the area around Cucuron has been continuously inhabited since prehistoric times.**

Contents

❧

RIGHT: All the flavors and colors of Provence, from eucalyptus to *coquelicot*, or "poppy," are concentrated in candies for sale at one of the region's most famous sites—Mont Ventoux, beloved of the great poet Petrarch.

PAGES 10–11: Twelve miles (19km) west of Avignon's bustling sophistication, the Pont du Gard arches across the wilderness of the Garrigue. The Roman general Agrippa ordered it built in the Roman fashion— without mortar—two thousand years ago to carry water to Nîmes. Following the withdrawal of Roman troops, the aqueduct was abandoned, its stones carried away for other construction projects. It was another general, Napoleon, who restored the ancient structure, which is now one of the region's most popular sites.

PART I

L'HISTOIRE

ACCORDING TO AN EARLY MEDIEVAL LEGEND, MARY MAGDALENE, THE PENITENT SINNER BELOVED OF JESUS (AND WHO WAS ONE OF HIS DISCIPLES), WAS SET ADRIFT FROM THE HOLY LAND IN A SMALL BOAT WITH OTHER SAINTS AND A "BLACK" SERVANT, SARAH. THE BAND OF TRAVELERS ARRIVED AT MARSEILLES (WHICH PAGAN CITY THE MAGDALENE LATER CONVERTED), AND THEN SEPARATED. MARY, THE MOTHER OF JAMES MINOR; MARY SALOME, THE MOTHER OF JAMES MAJOR AND JOHN; AND SARAH SETTLED IN THE CAMARGUE AND, WHEN THEY DIED, WERE BURIED THERE. THE RELICS OF THESE SAINTS ARE STILL TODAY OBJECTS OF FERVENT VENERATION; FOR TWO DAYS IN MAY, A ROMANY PILGRIMAGE VENERATES THE SAINTS, ESPECIALLY THE HUMBLE, DARK-SKINNED SARAH.

THE HISTORY OF PROVENCE IS RICH WITH SUCH WONDERS. IN THE TWELFTH CENTURY A SHEPHERD NAMED BÉNÉZET HAD A VISION DIRECTING HIM TO BUILD A BRIDGE OVER THE RHÔNE AT A POINT INDICATED BY AN ANGEL. AFTER OBTAINING PERMISSION FROM THE BISHOP OF AVIGNON, BÉNÉZET MIRACULOUSLY SOLVED ENGINEERING PROBLEMS THAT HAD DEFEATED EVEN THE ROMANS, AND THE BRIDGE OPENED IN 1188. THE PONT D'AVIGNON, WHICH ONCE BOASTED TWENTY-TWO PIERS, IS NOW DOWN TO FOUR AND NO LONGER SPANS THE RIVER. THE RING-DANCE FEATURED IN THE SONG TOOK PLACE NOT "ON" (*SUR*) THE BRIDGE, BUT "UNDER" (*SOUS*) IT, ON AN ISLAND IN MIDSTREAM.

❧

OPPOSITE: **A field dotted with poppies leads to a line of plane trees near Saint-Rémy-de-Provence. The geometries and colors of Provence attracted such artists as Vincent van Gogh, Paul Gauguin, and Paul Cézanne. Cézanne was born in Aix-en-Provence in 1839 and, like many painters, eventually found his way to Paris; in 1870, he left Paris and returned to Aix, where he would spend the second half of his life.**

Something in these tales resonates for the modern viewer, for Provence is a spiritual, magical place that effortlessly combines the earthly and the sublime in one of the most varied landscapes in the world. From remote, forbidding mountain peaks to fertile, billowing plains to sun-drenched beaches lapped by the waters of the Mediterranean, the region's diverse beauty is both brash and elusive. Yet despite all this visual splendor, Provence is most famous for a scent: from the hills of the Garrigue and the Vaucluse Plateau, fields of lavender release the signature fragrance of Provence into the air, softening sleep and tinting dreams. Likewise the celebrated "herbes de Provence"—thyme, rosemary, marjoram, basil, savory, and sage—crowd the region's markets and lend their sensual, complex flavors to the unmistakable, aromatic cuisine of the region. These scents have always been as essential to the identity of Provence as to its economy; when the cardinal Louis d'Aragon traveled through Europe in 1517 and 1518, his chronicler commented upon the marvelous scents that wafted from the land around Marseilles out to sea and the ship on which they traveled.

By way of contrast, there is also Provence's notorious mistral, the cold north-northwest wind that the Rhône Valley channels to the Mediterranean. The mistral determines much of the region's architecture, from the windowless north-facing walls of the *mas* (the typical Provençal farmhouses) to the cage-like bell towers that allow the wind to pass harmlessly through. The celebrated seventeenth-century letter-writer Madame de Sévigné, who spent much time visiting her daughter, the wife of a Provençal nobleman, described the mistral as "that bitter, freezing wind that cuts one's being to the quick." The mistral, which can blow up to 200 kph (125mph), is said to drive people and animals insane—its name derives from the Provençal word for "master."

Despite the area's sophistication and antiquity, Avignon's grandeur, urban avenues of eighteenth-century elegance, and the chic of the seaside towns, there is something disarming about Provence's day-to-dayness. It wears its long history—visible at every turn—gracefully. This easy charm is as characteristic of Provence as the unmistakable accent and wry humor of the region's natives. The Provençals manage to combine reserve and cordiality toward strangers, displaying a special warmth toward returning visitors and friends.

Provence's most famous sons and daughters range from the regal to the venal. Marguerite of Provence married King

Provence is famous for its benign climate, but equally characteristic is the mistral, a wind so powerful that bell towers, such as this one near Lacoste, are designed like cages to let the fierce northerly gusts pass through.

(and later Saint) Louis IX in 1234, before she was fourteen. Provence was her dowry, and it gave her husband Aigues-Mortes, the port he needed for the six years of the Seventh Crusade (which the pious couple undertook together). In 1552, the physician Michel de Nostredame, better known as Nostradamus, prophesied the manner of Henri II's death (at a tournament). His poetic work *Centuries* consists of rhymed predictions, many of which have been interpreted as applying to the twentieth century. Born in 1740, Comte Donatien-Alphonse-François, descendant of the lords of Lacoste, was first an army officer and, late in the century, an author of novels and plays. He spent much of his life in prison for sexual perversion, and especially for dosing his victims—most of them of the poorer classes—with the painful irritant known as Spanish fly. The so-called Marquis de Sade died in the notorious insane asylum of Charenton, outside of Paris, in 1814.

People have lived in this area continuously since the Middle Stone Age; the New Stone Age inhabitants left traces of pottery and agriculture from as early as about 6000 B.C.E. In the early sixth century B.C.E., driven by their homeland's inability to feed an increasing population, Greek traders from Phocaea, on the west coast of Asia Minor (today Turkey), founded Marseilles as a trading colony. The Greek occupation was an embattled one, although in time Marseilles, trading along the fertile Rhône Valley and up and down the coast, would eventually establish colonies of its own.

The indomitable resistance of the local people impelled the Greeks to seek military assistance from the Romans, who in the second century B.C.E. occupied the region, which was increasingly harassed by the onslaughts of invading Celts or Germans. Ever since the Roman consul Gaius Marius gained a definitive victory over the barbarian tribes at Aix-en-Provence in 102 B.C.E., it has been the custom for Provençal families to name one of their sons after him. The gratitude of the Provençals toward the Roman liberators is also evident in the popularity of the name César as well—movie lovers

The *mas* is the farmhouse of Provence. Here, a resident eyes the photographer from a fancifully decorated stable at the Mas de l'ange, "the mas of the angel."

will immediately think of Marcel Pagnol's enchanting film trilogy, *Marius*, *Fanny*, and *César*.

Julius Caesar conquered Gaul during the period from 58 to 52 B.C.E.; the region of the Rhône and Durance rivers and their deltas was a province of Rome by the end of the century. (Roughly the same now as then, Provence is bordered by the Mediterranean to the south, Alpine chains to the east and northeast, and by the Rhône on the west.) With its mild climate, prodigiously fertile soil, and natural beauty, it was immediately popular with aristocratic Romans, especially those who for various reasons found it advisable to be absent from Rome itself. So attractive was the area that, as one historian puts it, it was spoken of as "the province" (*provincia*)—hence its name. The ancient Roman influence remains visible

Gold, blue, and deep green are the hues of late summer in Provence, as the millennial mountain shadows rise like protective giants behind the golden sweep of wheatfields.

today, in architectural masterpieces such as the amphitheater in Arles, the temple in Nîmes, and the Arc de Triomphe in Carpentras, as well as in place names throughout the region, from Aigues-Mortes ("dead waters") to Vaison-la-Romaine. Yet older beliefs linger as well: Nîmes is a corruption of "Nemausus," the spirit of a local spring, and the name of Val-des-Nymphes, a tiny vale watered by many waterfalls, recalls the nature worship practiced by long-ago ancestors.

In the early Middle Ages, amid the desolation and terror of the barbarian invasions, rendered all the more bitter by fading memories of the prosperity of Arles and Marseilles, the monastery of the Ile des Lérins, off the coast at Cannes, was a beacon of learning, drawing students such as Saint Patrick, who would later be instrumental in the Christianization of Ireland.

Perhaps because Provence was so heavily traveled—lying as it does between Italy and Spain, and France and the sea—it experienced all the travails of the heresies and their suppression and of the sixteenth-century Wars of Religion. Still today, the populations of such towns as Dieulefit ("God made it") are primarily Protestant.

The traces of history and trade remain as well, in the richly varied crafts of Provence. The region's much-prized printed fabrics were originally products of an illegal industry that arose in the seventeenth century to imitate imported Indian cottons. Provençal pottery ranges from modest traditional creations in *terre rouge* ("red earth") to faïence, a decorative earthenware pottery introduced from Italy in the sixteenth century, to intricately glazed ceramics bearing the elegant,

unmistakable arabesques of Moorish design. The *santons*— crèche figures made only in Provence—reveal much of the history of the region and of France. These Nativity scenes, inspired by southern Italian models, first appeared in Roman Catholic churches as part of the Counter-Reformation's encouragement of popular piety. During the French Revolution, the newly secular government closed the churches, and artisans soon devised figures of clay or paper that families could afford to have in their homes. These figures came to reflect contemporary events, such as Napoleon's rise to power and the advent of the locomotive, and were often dressed in contemporary Provençal costume, which brought the ancient, sacred scene into everyday life.

Though the region was officially absorbed into the kingdom of France in 1486, its geography, history, language, and diverse cultural ties have kept Provence a place apart, with a strong sense of individuality and tradition. Its mountains did not deter early invaders from the north, such as the Germanic tribes and the Normans; indeed, because of its position on the Mediterranean, Provence also suffered invasions from the sea, from the Saracens and Moors. Sharing a coast with Italy, it also partook of an intense cultural exchange with the northern cities of that country; one of Italy's most important poets, Francesco Petrarca (1304–1374), lived in Avignon. There, in the best tradition of courtly love, he first saw and fell in love with "Laura," perhaps the wife of Hugues de Sade, Laure de Noves, who inspired some of his most beautiful works.

Because of its geographical situation, the region's dialect, Occitane, or the *langue d'oc*, developed independently from the *langue d'oïl*, spoken in the north (the names of the dialects were taken from the word for "yes" in each). The langue d'oc seemed to lend itself naturally to poetry and song; beginning in the eleventh century, the fashion of *courtoisie,* which originated in the Midi, the south of France, gave rise to the lays of courtly love. The tales of Arthur, Guinevere, and the knights of the Round Table came out of this tradition, as did the celebrated poems of Christine de Pisan and works by Giovanni Boccaccio and Geoffrey Chaucer. For the first time in recorded history in Europe, women—or, more precisely, aristocratic ladies—were admired and honored. The male troubadours and their female counterparts, the trobairitz, sang songs of (usually spiritual) passion between handsome and beautiful young lords and ladies. This may have been due to an increasingly fervent cult of the Virgin Mary, or a desire to stand apart from the Muslims, who—despite the Prophet Muhammad's revolutionary laws on behalf of women in the Koran—generally maintained the same institutionalized contempt for them that prevailed in Europe, and were shocked by what they perceived as women's domination at the Christian courts.

The first *chansons de gestes*, or epic poetry of a hero's great deeds, appeared in eighth-century France, following the death of Charlemagne; during the centuries of the Crusades these works became a major art form in southern Spain, southern France, and southern Italy, probably because these were the areas of Europe most directly in contact with the Saracens and Moors. So beautiful and so highly esteemed was Provençal in medieval Europe that Dante Alighieri considered using it for his *Divine Comedy*, one of the world's masterpieces.

The people of Provence have always felt pride in their language, not least because it stood as a living symbol of the region's long independence. In 1539, the kingdom of France made French the language of the region's administrative laws as part of the process of absorbing Provence into the kingdom. Little by little, the literary language dwindled as well, although the dialect survived in its spoken form. In 1854, a group of Provençal writers founded a literary circle, the Félibrige, to encourage the rebirth of the langue d'oc. One of this group's members, the poet and lexicographer Frédéric Mistral, shared the Nobel Prize for literature in 1904.

Typical of the Romanesque style are these ornate sculptures of the church in St. Saveur-sur-Tinée. The Tinée is the longest of the Var's tributaries.

The twelfth century was not only the golden age of Provençal poetry and song, but of architecture as well. A conservative synthesis of historic and local European styles resulted in a unique expression, the best examples of which decorate the cities of the Rhône Valley: the church of Saint Trophime in Arles, Old Major Cathedral in Marseilles, and Saint Gilles in Avignon, to name but a few. However, the handsome, imposing Palais des Papes in Avignon, built in the fourteenth century, is unique in the world. The popes had ruled from that city since 1309, in part because of the turmoil in Rome, the traditional city of the papacy; for more than a century—described by one historian as "the second Babylonian captivity of the Church"—Avignon was at the center of the fierce politics of the times. In 1377, Pope Gregory XI, largely persuaded by Catherine of Siena (later Saint Catherine), returned the papacy to Rome, but his successor was so controversial that the French cardinals in effect seceded, returned to France, and elected a pope of their own. The Great Schism culminated in the election of a third, compromise, pope. Finally, a Church council elected

a pope, after the three abdicated or were deposed; the Supreme Pontiff has resided in the Eternal City ever since. Nevertheless, Avignon remained papal property until the French Revolution.

The latest generations of invaders arrived by train and ocean liner, plane and yacht. In the late 1800s, a few of the groundbreaking modern artists left Paris for Provence. Of the artists famous today, Paul Cézanne was the first to move there, and his Cubist landscapes capture the delicate shades and contours of the countryside. Though Vincent van Gogh hungered for the region's warm sun and brilliant colors (and low cost of living), as the eternal outsider he was also attracted to the Félibrige and their devotion to the language and history of their homeland. It was one of his most cherished fantasies to one day be invited to join the celebrated collective. Henri Matisse made his home in Provence, mainly in Nice, for much of the last decades of his life, and Pablo Picasso, after summers in Juan-les-Pins, retired to the Riviera.

The Americans came, too: Hemingway and his ménage à trois, and the frantically glamorous Fitzgeralds. From the

This medieval fresco from the Palais des Papes in Avignon bespeaks the popes' temporal power and secular pastimes—hunting was reserved strictly for the nobility.

British commonwealth came Katherine Mansfield, Somerset Maugham, and Graham Greene, among countless others. The British sought the sun and the mild winters; the artists and writers sought their own kind. These seekers, outsiders in their native lands, made homes here, for a time or forever. Restless wanderers, they surrendered to the matter-of-fact welcome that awaits in every fold of Provence's changing landscape, in every twist of the region's secret, subtle depth and deceptive simplicity. Provence is endlessly diverse, first by geography, then by history, and finally by nature. And in its infinite variety lies both its elusive mystery, and its eternal present, as brilliant as a sunflower.

Mountains

The mountains are everywhere in Provence. Often remote and inaccessible, they have been inhabited—and uninhabited—for thousands of years. In the early Middle Ages, many people retreated from the barbarian invasions to the region's highest peaks, creating the famous *villages perchés*, "perched towns." In the last decades, many of these picturesque towns have been restored, and now are famous for their fine crafts, mouthwatering cuisine, and the stunning views that appear at almost every turn of the winding medieval streets.

These hills and mountains sheltered many of the medieval heretics. One of the most famous of these was Pierre Valdès, or Peter Waldo (died c.1218), who preached voluntary poverty and read from the Gospels in Provençal, the language of the people, rather than the Latin of the Roman Catholic Church. Valdès originally received the pope's qualified support, but he was later excommunicated, and his followers were persecuted. Over the next three centuries, the group's resistance was sometimes aggressive; they destroyed local churches and sacred objects in their stronghold in the Lubéron, the mountains of southeast Provence. In 1545, King Francis I launched a military campaign against these Waldenses, or Vaudois. Some twenty-five villages were destroyed, almost two thousand believers were put to death (some of them by stoning), and six hundred were condemned to the living death of the galleys. Those who managed to escape fled east, through the Alpes-Maritimes and the Alpes de Haute-Provence into the Swiss and Italian Alps, where enclaves survive to this day.

An extension of the Lubéron to the west is the Alpilles, a series of jutting crests between Arles and Avignon, whose highest peaks reach some twelve hundred meters (4,000ft). This range features the most spectacularly—and eerily—evocative of all the mountain villages: Les-Baux-de-Provence. The lower village is a charming, lively commercial town of shaded squares and handsome buildings, constructed from the thirteenth century to the present. The upper village, however, is a unique and breathtaking human experience. On a spur atop sheer cliffs rises the Ville Morte, or Dead Town.

The *seigneurs de Baux* were the epitome of the proud lords of the Middle Ages: they claimed to trace their ancestry back to Balthazar the Magus, one of the three Wise Men who followed

OPPOSITE: **The Mediterranean vegetation of Saint-Paul-de-Vence surrounds a deceptively humble home in the hills above the high-profile chic of Nice.**

the star of Bethlehem to the Nativity. As a sign of their proximity to the very origins of Christianity, they bore a star on their coat of arms. Beginning in the eleventh century, these powerful nobles, lords of many towns in the region, won—and married—great titles. The upper town, about one kilometer (.6mi) long and two hundred meters (656ft) wide, numbered six thousand inhabitants at its greatest flowering, and the palace of the lords of Baux was one of the celebrated "courts of love" in the days of the troubadours. The line died out in 1393, and the town was absorbed first into the county of Provence, then in 1486, into the kingdom of France. Les Baux was the king's to give, and for a time in the late 1500s, when it was held by the Manville family, the town was Protestant. In 1632, Louis XIII—or his cardinal, the duc de Richelieu—razed the town and, for extra measure, fined its inhabitants 100,000 livres. Some two hundred years later, bauxite (named for the town) was discovered nearby. The raw material of aluminum, it brought the lower village back to life. One of Provence's most picturesque festivals takes place in Les Baux at Christmas, when shepherds accompany a new-born lamb, in a small cart drawn by a ram, to the altar of Saint Vincent's church.

ABOVE: **More than a million visitors a year are drawn to the medieval ghost town of Les-Baux-de-Provence, high in the Alpilles. Even the inhabited town farther down the mountainside can be reached only by foot.**

The region's highest, most famous, and best-loved mountain is Mont Ventoux, the "windy peak." Reigning over the northeast of the region, this mountain's legendary views take in the Baronnies Plateau to the north, the Vaucluse Plateau to the south, and the Rhône Valley to the west. Its stripped white peak is equally dramatic whether it is reaching into a flawless blue Provençal sky or dauntlessly piercing lead-gray storm clouds. Below the high peak, the mountainsides are brilliant with white shingle; the harsh upper reaches slope down into gentle folds dressed in cypresses, evergreens, broom, and wild iris. In the summertime, the air is perfumed with the scent of cedar, wild rosemary, and thyme. Little is left of the forests that once blanketed Mont Ventoux—the trees were sacrificed to make the ships used in centuries of war and commerce.

The last foothills of the Ventoux mountain range scarcely look like foothills at all. The vertical peaks of the Dentelles de Montmirail were produced by a series of geological events: the upper layers of limestone were thrust upright when the Earth's crust folded, and millennia of rains and wind did the rest. Beaumes-de-Venise is an attractive terraced town on the southern slopes of the Dentelles, but it is the foothills to the west that draw oenophiles from the world over, for these are the vineyards of the Côtes-du-Rhône. Nestled among them are the villages whose names grace some of the most popular French wine labels: Gigondas, Sablet, and Séguret are only three of these. The Séguret vineyard is one of the area's most charming sites, with a twelfth-century church that features an array of santons at Christmastime.

According to her legend, after she converted the city of Marseilles, Mary Magdalene retired to a holy cave in the Sainte-Baume Massif, northeast of Marseilles, for thirty-three years—the length of time that Jesus was on Earth. She never ate, we are told, but lived solely on the songs of the heavenly hosts. When her time came to pass on, she called for Maximinus, her traveling companion of long ago, now a bishop; her face was so radiant that Maximinus could scarcely look at her. He gave Mary Magdalene Holy Communion, and "her soul took its flight to the Lord."

The name of the massif, the saint's cave, and the surrounding forest are all taken from *baumo*, the Provençal word for "cave." The French word *baume*, however, means "balm," and the Magdalen is often represented in art as holding a jar of balm, or ointment. When the wealthy Mary of Magdala repented her libertine ways, she washed Christ's feet and soothed them with ointment. She was also one of the women who prepared Christ's body for burial, with "sweet spices." Caves are resonant images as well in the life of the Great Penitent: Mary Magdalene remained at Christ's tomb—in fact, a burial cave—after the others had gone. So beloved was she by Jesus that she was the first to see the Risen Christ, and it was she who received from him the mission to tell the others of the miracle. Her life as a hermit in the cave of the massif recalls Christ's Passion, but also the eternal atonement of the cave-dwelling anchorites of her Near Eastern home. Still today, Mary's cave attracts the faithful, who come in pilgrimage—embraced by the dark of night, the spot becomes a holy site for midnight Mass on her feast day, July 22.

ABOVE: **A solitary farm building keeps watch in a fertile field of the Grand Lubéron.**

Plateaus

Say "Provence," and the Rhône Valley comes to mind, whether in Vincent van Gogh's preternaturally bright textured oils, or in Paul Cézanne's scrupulous Cubist landscapes, which seem to partake more of memory than observation. However its likeness has been interpreted, the Rhône was the conduit between the region and the outside world.

Arles—where van Gogh hoped to find a home, peace, and happiness—epitomizes the history of Provence. The city, today a handsome, lively town, was settled by the Greeks of Marseilles as a trading post on the river. In the second century B.C.E., Marius ordered a canal dredged to the coast at Marseilles. With each improvement, the volume of commerce increased, and the city prospered accordingly. In 49 B.C.E., Julius Caesar defeated Marseilles and gave a number of the

ABOVE: **A fountainhead in Arles shows Hercules in a lionskin; of course, the worship of sacred springs is far older than the Olympian gods.**

city's possessions to Arles; he further established a colony for his Sixth Legion. Many of the public buildings—including an amphitheater, in which medieval inhabitants built a township of two hundred homes—survive today.

Arles was on the Aurelian Way, the imperial road between Italy and Spain, as well as on roads to northern and western Gaul. The city thrived—it became the second wealthiest city of the Roman empire after Rome itself, and was home to the imperial mint. Constantine built a palace there, which survives today, and a bridge across the river; in 314 C.E., the emperor held the first Council of Christian Bishops in Arles.

In the fifth century, an awed visitor reported: "All that the Orient, unguent Araby, luxuriant Assyria, fertile Africa, Spain, and fecund Gaul produce is to be found in Arles and in as great quantity as in their countries of origin." The city's commercial connections by road and water also fed the region's manufacturers of fabrics and armor, and gold- and silverwork, with raw materials. The cathedral of Saint-Trophime, which already existed in the late sixth century, was built to honor the Greek saint who, legend has it,

converted much of Provence. The twelfth-century cloisters are a masterpiece of Provençal architecture and sculptural decoration—one of the later Gothic galleries, from the fourteenth century, displays local legends carved in stone. Van Gogh painted the nearby Alyscamps several times, rendering the ancient cemetery with a perhaps wistful serenity. Originally a Roman burial ground, it was used as late as the Middle Ages, when it was one of Europe's best known cemeteries.

Van Gogh was enchanted with the blooming peach and almond trees. Today a characteristic sight in the environs of Arles, they were originally imported from the Orient in the sixteenth century, perhaps to make up for the confections no longer coming from Spain (an unfortunate consequence of the expulsion of the Moors). Almond trees were propagated throughout Provence, especially in the Ardèche, in northwestern Provence, and into the Vaucluse Plateau. The nuts were mixed with the local honey according to the makers' secret recipes, and the result was nougat (Old Provençal for "nut"). Montélimar, in the Ardèche, sells the most famous nougat, although much is now mass-produced. Tiny Sault,

Orange's celebrated Roman theater, generally considered the finest and best-preserved example of its kind, was built in the reign of the emperor Augustus. More than fifteen hundred years later, its wall was admired by the Sun King, Louis XIV.

high above the western edge of the Vaucluse Plateau, claims to make the best.

One of the strangest areas in Provence is the Crau Plain. In the mid-sixteenth century, a canal was dug that made possible the irrigation and cultivation of the Petite Crau, east of Arles. Edged with poplar and cypress, the Petite Crau is home to fruit orchards and fields of vegetables, and in the winter sheep graze the fourth (and last) of the year's hay crops. To the south stretches the Grande Crau, one of the most unforgiving deserts in the world, a gray and white expanse of gravel and shingle so awesome that it is mentioned in myth; as the story goes, Hercules was on his way to Spain when he was confronted by a group of Ligurian warriors. After

shooting all his arrows, the hero called upon his father, Jupiter, to assist him. The king of the gods showered his son's enemies with rocks and stones, creating the strata of the Grande Crau (which in places is as deep as 15 meters [50ft]).

Below Sault, the vast Vaucluse plain is planted in lavender. In high summer, when the heat and sun have muted the myriad colors of Provence, the aromatic herb's pale gray-violet surprises the observer with the lingering, sensuous intensity of its perfume. In mid-August, at harvest time, every street, courtyard, and corner of town is filled with fragrance.

Also on the Vaucluse Plateau, to the southeast, are Roussillon and Rustrel Colorado. What the lavender fields are to scent, this area of ocher quarries is to sight. Used for centuries as housepaint, ocher occurs naturally in as many as seventeen distinct shades, from crimson to van Gogh–sunflower-yellow. Though several of the quarries are exhausted, the houses of Roussillon display the brilliant range of nature's prodigal palette.

The grandest city of the Rhône Valley, and perhaps of all Provence, is Avignon. The coincidence of the rise of the papacy's secular power and the popes' transfer to France resulted in the astonishing architecture of the Popes' Palace. Its imposing, perfectly preserved walls rise red-gold against the pale blue of the southern sky; the interior is a winding medieval labyrinth of vast, decorated halls. In the seventeenth and eighteenth centuries, an artistic and architectural revival enriched the city's churches with religious painting and sculpture, and the urban fabric with elegant town houses.

The town of Roussillon is a showcase for the myriad hues of ocher—earth blended with hydrated oxide of iron and other materials—mined in the region. This traditional wall treatment warms up a modern architectural design.

It is Avignon's special grace to create an elegant harmony out of its many and diverse parts—its magic, that you could not imagine it different than what it is. The warm sun of autumn seems to carry autumn's colors within it, mellowing the high, perfect walls of the Palais des Papes to the color of red-gold. Across the Rhône from the Palais, low, inscrutable hills undulate on the western horizon. The old town is a gentle maze, within which nestle small squares, surprises to urban wanderers who drift down the narrow streets between homes three or four stories high. Here, historical periods merge into an unpredictable unity: the shabby gentility of eighteenth-century town houses beside restored homes of two centuries before. The city's architectural intimacy is infectious, endowing its inhabitants with a subdued, seductive individuality that courses through every exchange, whether among shopkeepers and shoppers, or families, friends, and lovers.

Sea

Even the coastline of Provence is wondrously varied, from the sites of seaside luxury on the Côte d'Azur—the "sky-blue coast"—to the wildlife preserves of the Camargue and the medieval bastions of Aigues-Mortes. Marseilles' rough reputation is not unjustified, but in the main it shares the same mythic roots as all seaports, which are perceived to be populated with transient, rootless wanderers, have-nots with nothing to lose. One of the most active ports of the Mediterranean, and the largest city in Provence, Marseilles receives many immigrants from the southern Mediterranean, a phenomenon

that tends to ignite reactionary fears and phobias. And indeed the National Front is a presence in Marseilles. Of course, for the most part, the city, like the more traditional towns in the interior, continues to vote socialist, while Nice and Cannes, the wealthier cities of the Côte d'Azur, tend to be right-wing.

Ancient historians recount that when the Phocaeans arrived on these shores in 600 B.C.E., they attended a banquet given by the local Ligurian chieftain in honor of his daughter, who was to choose her husband from among those present. She chose Protis, the Phocean commander, and her dowry was the hill behind Marseilles.

During Julius Caesar's occupation of Gaul, politics was Marseilles' near downfall, when the city backed Pompey during Rome's civil war. Caesar pauperized the city, distributing its wealth and his favor to Arles and Narbonne, among other cities. Like most of Europe, Marseilles was devastated by the recurring barbarian invasions and the plague; like most of the northern Mediterranean port towns, it suffered from constant Saracen attacks. But also like the port cities, it flourished as a result of the Crusades, first as a port from which the Crusaders sailed, and later as a merchant city with its own quarter in Jerusalem.

According to legend, when the Holy Marys, who had been set adrift from the Holy Land after the Crucifixion, landed at Saintes-Maries-de-la-Mer, the Magdalene and her brother, Lazarus, went to Marseilles; after she converted the city and retired to the life of a hermit in the Sainte-Baume, he remained.

During the French Revolution, a contingent of five hundred volunteers marched to Paris, singing the song that

became the anthem of the Revolution itself and will forever recall the fervent volunteers: "La marseillaise." Some one hundred years later, film history was made down the coast to the east, at La Ciotat, the location of what may have been the first moving picture, *Arrival of a Train into La Ciotat Station*, by the Lumière brothers. Marseilles would make architectural history as well, with Le Corbusier's radical 1952 design for an apartment building that would incorporate its own "shopping street" and social center for the residents. Le Corbusier's original plan for his Cité Radieuse, or Radiant City, called for an arrangement of six buildings, but the much disputed project was halted after just one was built. Marseilles, almost alone in this regard among the cities of Provence, retains little of its past, except in certain narrow streets of its old

More than twenty-five hundred years ago, Greek ships sailed into Massilia, present-day Marseilles, one of France's largest and oldest cities. This picturesque but unassuming corner of the city retains the feel of a Mediterranean village.

quarter, or in ancient churches tucked away amid the city's modern growth.

West of Marseilles's bustling streets, which are scented at midday with its aromatic cuisine (rich with tomatoes, saffron, and spicy ground pepper), is the enigma of the Camargue, the lagoons of the Rhône delta. In its mysterious light, this marshland seems to ceaselessly shift its identity, becoming in turn sea, land, and air, just as its vegetation turns green, gray, and red over the course of the seasons. Here are wild boar and flamingos and other marsh birds. Wild horses run here, and it is home to the famous bulls used for the *cocarde*, the Provençal bullfight, in which prowess, not death, is celebrated.

This is the region of Saintes-Maries-de-la-Mer, the place where the Holy Marys were said to have landed. While the Magdalene and Lazarus went to Marseilles, Maximinus to Aix, and Martha to Tarascon—where she defeated a river monster with the sign of the cross—the mothers of three apostles stayed here with their servant, Sarah, the Gypsies' patron saint. For at least five hundred years Romany tribes have gathered from all over Europe, making the pilgrimage to this tiny port on May 24

and 25. A second pilgrimage takes place in October, attended only by *gadjos* (non-gypsies).

In the desolate reaches of the Camargue, at the western edge of Provence, lies Aigues-Mortes. Its name, meaning "dead waters" in Latin, reflects the superstitious awe that the Camargue has perhaps always inspired. Aigues-Mortes is a sleeping city whose enchanted dreams were interrupted only once—and briefly, at that—in the thirteenth century.

In 1240, Louis IX—who was canonized less than thirty years after his death—began to prepare to go on a Crusade. His wife, Margaret, brought Provence to the alliance, and the monastery of the Camargue gave him this town, at that time little more than a settlement of a handful of fishermen. Louis built the Constance Tower, began construction of the ramparts, and granted privileges to the town to attract new residents. (In the fourteenth century, Aigues-Mortes would count some fifteen thousand inhabitants, a significant figure considering that Florence, one of the largest cities in Europe, had 100,000 residents only a century later.) The ardent king set sail for the Seventh Crusade in 1248; he was taken and ransomed in Egypt, and returned to France

The sea gives up its silver (in this case, mackerel) today as it has for centuries, forming the basis of the south's unique cuisine, which like the region itself, brilliantly combines heartiness, subtlety, and spice. One of the signature dishes of the region is the world-famous fish stew known as bouillabaisse.

in 1254 after an unsuccessful campaign in Palestine. In 1270, he embarked on the Eighth Crusade, sailing to Tunis, where he died of the plague. His son, the perhaps sarcastically nicknamed Philip the Bold, completed the walls of the city. The Crusades came to an end, and gradually the port of Aigues-Mortes silted up. Eastward, at the opposite end of the Provence coast, Marseilles continued to thrive, as all the wealth of the region flowed through it, and it rejoined the network of Mediterranean ports. Time slowed in Aigues-Mortes, and the young people left, as the Camargue claimed the town once more. The port ceased to be. Today, five thousand souls—one third the number of five hundred years ago—inhabit the wall-girded town that rises like memory among the marshes and lagoons.

are the descendants of sailors who plied the ports of antiquity, farmers who nurtured the land and coaxed treasures from the soil, conquerors who took their ease among the region's comforts, kings and queens, and poets, painters, and writers; its legends are those of the Gypsies, the world's outcasts, who met in Provence to honor a servant-saint, as well as the legends of the Bible.

Provence is also a feast of the senses: the scents of hay, sage, and lavender; the golds of ocher, Avignon, and sunflowers; the blues of the sky over Mont Ventoux and of the sea beyond Aigues-Mortes, whence a king set sail for a saint's death. It is the shouts of the *gardians*, the cowboys of the Camargue; the voices of neighbors in the marketplace; and the memories of courtly love songs threading through the ruins of Les Baux, borne on the breeze. It is the echoes of languages that are no more, yet survive in the living language of this place, created to express what no other tongue can. Provence, unique and various, severe and splendid, rises from the enchanted past, as timeless and alive today as ever.

Fin

Provence is a living paradox, at the same time both simple and complex: its hundreds of cities and towns perch on remote mountain peaks and lounge along the azure coast; its people

The ancient mystery of the remote Camargue and its wild horses endures... The cherished tale of the three Maries and their companions lives on in the name of the principal town of these lagoons: Saintes-Maries-de-la-Mer.

PART II

LES
IMAGES

❧

PAGES 32–33: **The heart of Provence's magic is agricultural. These sunflowers, in a field near Arles, are descendants of the blooms that brought van Gogh joy in his final years.**

ABOVE: **Lavender is an herb of many pleasures, its scent equally at home in kitchen, bath, or bedroom.**

RIGHT: **An isolated canyon in the Vaucluse encloses Sénanque Abbey, founded in 1148 and occupied continuously by the Cistercians until the French Revolution, then on and off until 1969. With its orderly rows of lavender, the Abbey looks very much as it must have when it was home to the twelfth-century monks of this severe Benedictine rule.**

The brilliant red of the poppy is the universal Mediterranean accent. Long-used by herbalists to assuage pain and bring healing sleep, the flower has petals as delicate as butterfly wings, which belie its sturdy growth. Here, a tranquil, poppy-dotted field contrasts with the image conjured by the name of nearby Oppède, from the Latin word for "stronghold."

A swath of yellow mustard in flower recalls the antiquity of herbs and spices. Originally an essential part of religious ritual, these fragrant leaves, roots, barks, and fruits became prized in the Mediterranean region for their magical and medicinal properties and for their ability to preserve precious foods through seasons of scarcity.

ABOVE: **Gnarled and nightmarish in appearance, generous and benign in their fruit, these venerable grapevines of the Lubéron will produce some of the world's best-loved wines.**

RIGHT: **The orchards of Provence were beloved by van Gogh, who planned a seasonal cycle of paintings that he never completed. The Greeks, who founded colonies in Provence, also introduced the olive trees that have been an essential part of the region's landscape for millennia. In early winter, the leaves will turn silver.**

LEFT: Olives must be handpicked before all the fruit is ripe and kept in well-ventilated containers. Here, old (wicker) meets new (plastic), updating an age-old ritual...

ABOVE: A lavish display of peppercorns in an Arles market transports us back to the region's days of trade with the eastern Mediterranean, when such a rich array would have represented a king's ransom.

OPPOSITE: The abundance of Provence is represented in miniature in this restored farmhouse's opulent garden, near Grasse (the perfume capital of France), from cutting flowers to herbs to vegetables, and topiary, too.

ABOVE: **Saint-Michel-de-Frigolet Abbey, between Arles and Avignon, was founded in the tenth century as a sanitarium for the monks from nearby Montmajour Abbey, who came down with fevers while draining the marshes around their mother house. During the French Revolution, Saint-Michel-de-Frigolet was confiscated, only to be a monastery once more some fifty years later. Here, the twelfth-century cloister provides peace for contemporary contemplation.**

RIGHT: **A twelfth-century shepherd boy, obeying a divine command, succeeded in spanning the Rhône where the best Roman engineers had failed (though, alas, Saint Bénézet did not live to see the Pont d'Avignon open in 1188).**

ABOVE: **Riez, a tiny village not far from the Grand Canyon du Verdon, remains unspoiled, even though visitors have been coming for millennia in search of the region's lavender and honey, which are understandably world-famous. It remains so idyllic, perhaps, because in Riez commerce takes second place to neighborliness.**

BELOW: **A visitor attracts a child's frank curiosity in Ménerbes.**

ABOVE: **A woman, her face a study in time and character, watches the world go by in Saint-Rémy, her pet rooster by her side. Gaulish Celts, Greeks, and Romans lived in this area, but the town's two most famous inhabitants were the Renaissance seer Nostradamus and the doomed painter Vincent van Gogh.**

LEFT: The Palais des Papes is one of Europe's most imposing edifices, marrying the defenses dictated by medieval warfare with the splendor of the early Renaissance papal court. Graceful ogival arches lighten the courtyard walls, recalling the worldly culture that flowered at the papal residence.

BELOW: The palace retains its medieval essence in vaulted arches and massive stone flooring.

ABOVE: Arles' singular style is evident in this stretch of street, with its perfectly groomed homes decorated with subdued hues and such restrained aristocratic touches as marble and stone door and window frames.

❧

LEFT: Vincent van Gogh passed through this vaulted entrance to the hospital of Saint-Paul-de-Mausole, in Saint-Rémy, hoping for relief of his psychic pain. Here, as everywhere, he drew and painted what he saw.

BELOW: A loving hand has painted a quintessential Provençal landscape, rich with the golden yellow of wheat fields and the silver-violet haze of lavender. This fragrant flower is a specialty of the store that bears this charming sign.

LEFT: **Saint-Rémy, like many Provençal towns, still celebrates the cycles of the seasons with popular festivals that bring alive the primordial rhythms of farming and herding. The** *Fête de la transhumance* **marks the movement of sheep from their winter to their summer pastures.**

OPPOSITE: **In a street in Saint-Rémy, a run-down bicycle dreams of long-ago journeys.**

꘏

ABOVE: A *santonnier* carves a small statue representing one of
the traditional figures of the Nativity scene. Santons are a
specialty in several parts of Provence.

RIGHT: Terra-cotta tiles, biscuit-colored stone, and lush greens
of fields and hillside forests have cohabited for centuries.
This scene distills the essence of Provence.

LEFT AND BELOW: **Nestled in the remote forests of the Haut-Var, deep in its millennial dream, the twelfth-century Cistercian Abbaye du Thoronet, a vestige of the great days of monasticism, is the earliest of the three great Cistercian abbeys known as the "three Provençal sisters." The gentle Romanesque arches (opposite) of the cloister and window (below) are in perfect harmony with the spare serenity of this spiritual oasis.**

The majestic rock of Les Baux-de-Provence looks down over neatly trimmed olive trees. By moonlight, the winding streets and tiny squares of the ruined fortress seem alive again with the lords, ladies, soldiers, artisans, and families who populated the once-thriving town, its palace renowned for its troubadours and its court of love.

OPPOSITE: **Snow dusts the Alpilles and mantles the vineyards, a factor in the unique flavor of the next year's vintage...**

ABOVE: **Even in winter, the sun of Provence warms all colors. With painterly assurance, the composite house of Domaine Richeaume, a vineyard, sports a rich pink that sets off the deep, sober green of neighboring cypresses.**

ABOVE: The Pénitents des Mecs are a geological formation unique to Provence, and a mecca for hikers in the spring, when the yellow blossoms of broom brighten the sheer gray peaks.

LEFT: **The Dentelles de Montmirail rise in the Vaucluse. The name of this geological eccentricity derives from** *dents,* **or "teeth"—that is, the pins around which lacemakers work thread to make their delicate product, or** *dentelle.*

OPPOSITE: **The sinuous, improbably turquoise waters of the Verdon flow down through the mountains of Haute-Provence to pour into the Durance.**

BELOW: **Close by the Grand Canyon du Verdon, a courtyard in Moustiers-Sainte-Marie provides a tranquil outcropping of civilization.**

❧

ABOVE: **Weather-worn and handsome, this building façade in Sospel displays details of time, from a clock to a streetlamp to a religious image of the Lamb of God.**

❧

BELOW: **In the long shadows of a sultry Provence Larousse afternoon, a game of *boules* requires attention and precision.**

OPPOSITE: **The houses of Roussillon cling to its slope in the Vaucluse. In the foreground are outcroppings of the ocher that has been used to decorate the outside walls of houses since time immemorial.**

RIGHT: **A steep cobblestone street in Gordes leads up to a medieval house, whose almost windowless ground floor testifies to the reality of that battle-ridden age.**

OPPOSITE: **Olive trees and vineyards—the long-ago gifts of the Greeks—are the vital vegetation of the Mediterranean. In the higher reaches of the Alpilles, the Provençal sun develops the precious fruits' complex flavors.**

ABOVE: **Spring explodes into blossoms on fruit trees and tender new leaves on grapevines. Each day's climate will affect the vintage's flavor, rendering it utterly individual.**

LEFT: The Riviera, with its crowds and
beaches, begins in the *département* of
the Var, yet the diverse natural beauty of
Provence is equally well represented.
Here, a house sits in poetic solitude in
the wooded uplands.

OPPOSITE: Just east of the Var, the Côte d'Azur
comes into its own in towns and cities
such as Cannes and Nice. In the hills above,
celebrities achieve the greatest of all luxuries—
peace and silence. Picasso, the archetypal
art star, created his studio within the
Château Grimaldi (pictured here),
just above Antibes' old town.

LEFT: Châteauneuf-du-Pape, literally "the pope's new castle," is one of France's best-known wine-growing regions. The prized grapes of this part of the Côtes-du-Rhône are said to have been planted originally by the Avignon pontiffs during the "second Babylonian captivity." Wine made here is jealously protected by the *appellation controlée* that appears on its labels.

BELOW: In the Alpilles, spring's tender hues are set off by the vigorous new growth in the fields behind.

OPPOSITE: Young grapevines in the alps of the Côte d'Azur seem to emit sunlight into a late spring mist.

❦

ABOVE: Perhaps nowhere in Provence is the region's characteristic contrast more arresting than between the Côte d'Azur and, just inland, the Massif des Maures, Provence's most ancient mountains. Virtually uninhabited, these hinterlands are made of a rock that absorbs light, rather than reflecting it, so that the landscape seems bathed in an otherworldly chiaroscuro. The name of the range comes from the Provençal *mauro*, meaning "dark," but also meaning Moor, recalling the North African Muslim invasions of the ninth century.

RIGHT: The plateaus of the Lubéron range are some of the most fertile in France. Here, an ancient patchwork of plantings extends into the mist.

❧

LEFT: Below the sheltering geology of the Dentelles, arcs of grapevines form an amphitheater of ripening promise.

TOP AND ABOVE: Wine-growing is as much a craft as wine-making, and the prized wines of Provence are marketed worldwide. Once an area of small vineyards, with the best vintages reserved for the Avignon popes and the nobility, Provence was planted intensively in the first decades of the twentieth century to provide the French soldiers of World War I with their ration of a liter a day.

PAGES 78–79: **To climb the precipitous streets of Saorge, a striking *village empilé* (stacked village) in the Alpes-Maritimes, is to live an experience like no other. As you pass beneath an arch formed by two adjacent homes, you might hear, woven into the town's Provençal and French, words from pre-Roman times...**

ABOVE: **A tree-lined street in Aix-en-Provence recalls the legend that Gothic cathedrals were inspired by forests. A native of Aix, Paul Cézanne returned there to pursue his artistic journey after his days in Paris.**

The sun reaches down into the narrow, cobblestone streets of the Panier (Basket) Quarter in Marseilles. The deep sills, embellished with geraniums to keep the mosquitoes away, reveal the thickness of walls meant to keep summer's heat at bay.

PAGES 82–83: Provence's wealth and strength have always been the region's agriculture, luring raiders in centuries past; of course, today's invaders tend to bring riches in, rather than take them away. Here, a sample of the variety of summer's harvests are piled high in markets of the cities and towns along the Côte d'Azur. The region's abundance of produce is still a matter of heartfelt pride today, proof perhaps of the enduring wisdom of taking pleasure in the everyday.

❧

LEFT: **Along the Grande Corniche, above the Côte d'Azur, below the castle of Roquebrune, a tumble of roofs shelters the maze of the fifteenth-century town of the same name.**
Not far to the east lies the Italian border.

BELOW: **Every fish counts—in Marseilles's Old Port, the nets can be mended by hand only, to ensure that the precious prey does not escape.**

✧

ABOVE: An urbane late-nineteenth-century wrought-iron lamppost in Saint-Tropez is a reminder of the village's sudden vault to *fin-de-siècle* stardom.

LEFT: The *calanques*, or inlets between steep ridges west of Cassis, are havens of turquoise waters, white cliffs, and peace.

OPPOSITE: Until one hundred years ago, the French Riviera, with the bustling exception of Marseilles, was a string of sleepy fishing villages. There was a time when its few visitors could only reach the remote, decidedly unglamorous village of Saint-Tropez by boat. Guy de Maupassant, novelist and *bon vivant*, arrived by yacht, the harbinger of other travel-hungry artist-celebrities.

ABOVE AND OPPOSITE: **One can sail or walk from Marseilles to the calanques—here, Port Miou (above) and Sugiton (opposite)—and imagine Greek, Roman, and Saracen ships on the horizon, or even an explorer's galleon hugging the coast before venturing westward out of the Mediterranean, and into the unknown.**

꧁

BELOW AND RIGHT: **For a few days in the spring and autumn, Saintes-Maries-de-la-Mer comes alive with a *gitan* (gypsy) pilgrimage and a blessing of the sea. The two-day ceremony in honor of the Maries has remained unchanged since the Middle Ages and is attended by people from throughout the area, from Arlésiens and Arlésiennes in traditional costume to the *gardians* on horseback. It is one of the very few places that Vincent van Gogh visited during his fateful last years in the Midi.**

RIGHT: **Overlooking the picturesque Baie des Fourmis, Beaulieu (for "beautiful spot," appropriately enough) revels in its sheltered position, enjoying one of the balmiest microclimates on the heavenly Riviera.**

PAGE 96: **As deep as time itself, and as constantly renewed, the hues of Provence are uniquely wild, rich, and subtle.**

PHOTO CREDITS

**PRINCIPAL PHOTOGRAPHY BY
GAIL MOONEY:**
Pages 7, 9, 10-11, 16, 18, 19, 21, 22, 25
right, 26-27 both, 30, 32-33, 34-35 both,
38 right-39, 40, 41 right, 42 left, 46-47
both, 52-53 both, 54-55 left, 60-61 both,
62-63 both, 65 left, 66, 70-71 both, 72
left, 74 left, 76-77 left, 78-79, 80, 82, 83
top both, 84-85 left, 86, 87 right, 88, 92-
93, 96

All other photography:
Corbis: ©Owen Franken: p. 77 right both

©**Howard Dinin:** p. 83 bottom

©**John Elk, III:** pp. 4-5, 42 right-43, 48,
67

©**Hugh Palmer:** p. 14

Scope: ©Jacques Guillard: pp. 15, 29, 41
left, 50, 56-57, 58-59 both, 65 right, 68-
69 both, 72 right, 81, 85 right, 87 left,
89, 90 left; ©Nathalie Pasquel: p. 31;
©Noel Hautemaniere: pp. 90 right-91

Tony Stone Images: ©Thomas Renaut:
pp. 1, 73; ©Denis Waugh: pp. 2-3;
©Robert Stahl: p. 51; ©David Epperson: p.
64; ©David C. Tomlinson: pp. 74 right-75,
endpapers

©**Stephen Trimble:** pp. 6, 13, 24-25 left,
36-37 both, 38 left, 44-45 all, 49 both,
55 right